Alex & Gabi Go West
INSIGHTS REVEALED

JORGE F. CASSIR, MD

Print information available on the last page

Rev. date: 05/19/2017

To order additional copies of this book, contact:
Xlibris
1-888-795-4274
www.Xlibris.com
Orders@Xlibris.com

If you want to raise a child that thrives joyfully, is disciplined, loving, kind, and makes you proud, this book is for your child and you. This is the author's second book and builds on the values and principles outlined in his previous book, *Baby Comes Home.* A child is born into this world with the full Essence, or "Spiritual Software," to unfold with ease and grace, into the highest expression of his/her Soul. Always confident in the knowledge that the love in his/her heart will be the only validation that he/she will ever need, never having to seek it in the outside world. Read and apply this book, then delight witnessing as your child grows and prospers free from the fears, self-doubt, anguish, anger, jealousies, and emotional and psychological burdens that afflict so many of the youth and adults in our country and our world."

—Derek Rydall, transformational coach and best-selling author of *Emergence: 7 Steps for Radical Life Change*

"This book is insightful. It lays the foundation towards strong parent-child bonding that will enrich their lives, and change the world."

—Datta Groover (President and Chief Happiness Officer) & Rachael Jayne Groover (CEO and Director of Vision and Alignment), Groover Seminars, Inc.

PREFACE

This is the second illustrated book in a series on spirituality in children. They are meant to be used by parents, and others, to make sure that their children grow up feeling secure and joyful, as conscious conduits in the manifestation of their Soul's dreams, to allow their spirit to flow freely without constraints in the creation of their own lives; to become beacons of light that will guide others and illumine the path of our human evolution.

All life on earth, when it sprouts, comes with the essence to be what it is meant to be. Children are born with the Essence to be human beings. They have Souls, and physical bodies, and minds. Our Souls are part of the same Spirit or Intelligence, the "God," that created our Universe billions of years ago. Our Souls remain with us, unchanged until we leave this planet. They are eternal and infinite; they are the source of all the love, light, knowledge, and abundance that we all need. There is no need for us to look outside of ourselves to live our destinies.

Since children are born with all the intelligence of the Universe, it is not necessary to "talk down" to them. The basic messages of love, warmth, tenderness, kindness, spontaneity, joy, and awe are easy for them to understand, as well as to express, by the way we look at them, talk to them, kiss them, touch them, embrace them, and rock and sing to them. They learn by seeing, touching, tasting, listening, and playing; by their parents reading to them; and by being avid observers and absorbers of all that surrounds them.

This book uses enriching words, observations, insights, and reflections that speak to and enrich the human Soul, which creates the miraculous and blissful orchestration of all aspects of our magical existence as finite beings and infinite Spiritual individuations of God.

Parents' Guide

Parents and other caregivers should read the story of Alex and Gabi thoughtfully and patiently, explaining to the child gradually over a period of time the meanings of the words that they may not be aware of and the messages or concepts that they may not fully comprehend. At first, it is more important to read it straight through so that they get the essence of the story. It's meant to be read repeatedly over a period of a few years until its basic spiritual concepts are clearly anchored in the child's consciousness. This is not a religious book. It is based on spiritual principles shared by all humanity: love, kindness, compassion, peace, harmony, gratitude, forgiveness, generosity, tolerance, and respect for all of life including animals, vegetation, and the environment.

By engaging with their children in this and other spiritual experiences, parents are not only rediscovering their higher selves but bonding with their little ones in very profound ways that enrich everybody's lives.

ALEX AND GABI GO WEST

The news of the birth of Emi's baby sister in California spread fast near and far. Alex and Gabi, two cousins from New York City, called Emi to congratulate her and her parents on the arrival of the new baby sister, and told her that they would come to visit.

Several weeks later, Alex, six years old, and sister Gabi, four years old, went to the airport to take an airplane to Los Angeles, California. It was a nice sunny day, and they were excited about their new adventure.

But before they got on board they had to go through security.

They then boarded the plane, which their mommy had explained to them was a "huge mechanical bird" with large engines to power the flight. Airplanes, unlike birds, cannot flap their wings to create the airlift needed for flight; they get it from their powerful engines.

When they had boarded, their mommy and daddy made sure that Alex and Gabi had window seats and each had a parent sitting next to them. They wanted to make sure that the children appreciated the wonderful miracle of flight,

They admired the beautiful scenery and the vastness of the sky, experienced the fun of soaring above the clouds, and marveled at the magnificence of Planet Earth. Our Home. Our Planetary Spaceship!

It was a very smooth flight during which Alex and Gabi experienced the magic of flying and were thrilled that they could almost touch the sky! Having enjoyed the great panoramas that the Earth and the heavens had to offer, a last celestial surprise awaited them as they were about to land: a magnificent huge sunset – a palette of fiery colors conveying enormous power, deep inspiration, and reverence. An overwhelming sense of joy filled their young hearts at the spectacular scenery. Alex said, "Look, how awesome!" Even little Gabi could not help feeling that they were in the presence of something really special. "Amazing!" she exclaimed. "The hand of GOD!" their daddy said.

Following a smooth landing they collected their luggage and took a cab to their hotel in Beverly Hills and checked in. Because it was early evening, and the baby had been put down to bed for the night, they decided to visit the next day and to go out for dinner after unpacking.

They went to a new restaurant that served healthy organic cuisine. Alex and Gabi's mommy made sure they ordered enriching foods. As she always reminded them, "You are what you eat."

"We are what we eat."
Eat Healthy

Everybody had miso soup, a nice fresh salad, and fish with herbs and plenty of vegetables. They also ordered fresh fruit drinks. After dinner they took a half-hour walk and then returned to the hotel.

Then they got ready for bed. They changed into their pajamas and gathered in the children's room to thank God for a wonderful day, for their family, and for all the love and abundance in their lives. Then they hugged each other and said in one voice, "We love one another!"

The next morning after breakfast Alex and Gabi called up Emi. They were very anxious to see her and meet their new baby cousin. Their family took a cab to Emi's house. It was a sunny day and the red apples on the apple trees in the front of the house seemed very yummy.

They went indoors and were greeted by a chorus of wildly joyous singing birds. The commotion woke up the baby and she flashed a welcoming smile, her invitation to play. After caressing and kissing the baby, the cousins presented the baby with a pink blanket with "Angel" embroidered in gold thread, and some rattles. And Emi received a talking doll.

Then the cousins and their parents went to the playpen to play with the baby. They sang lullabies accompanied by the melodious birds joining in jubilant rhythms that filled the room with happiness and love. The baby seemed so blissful that Emi said, "The baby seems to be in another world!" An insightful observation.

When it was time to feed the baby, Gabi asked if she could do it. Emi showed her how to hold the bottle, and then it was Alex's turn. The baby was happy, smiling, and touching the children's faces, expressing tender love. The parents congratulated the children for a well done job. And they felt proud to be trusted.

Next it was time for lunch. Everyone delighted in a tasty, aromatic lunch. It included yummy red apples from the garden. In the meantime the baby enjoyed the music of soothing lullabies as she swung in her musical chair with the chirping birds, touching everyone's heart.

After a delicious lunch and serenade, they walked to a nearby park – an amazing sensorial experience – a rainbow, colorful flowers of different kinds, elegant trees, a warm sun, and a caressing breeze. First they visited a huge garden that was a mini paradise with beautiful scented flowers, gorgeous dancing butterflies, and various other life forms including bees, ants, and centipedes. Everyone was in awe of mother nature.

Then it was time for free play, running around, kicking a soccer ball, and the seesaw. After that came the slide and the jungle gym. Meanwhile the baby was transfixed, absorbing all of the action and approvingly beaming a beautiful smile. Emi blurted out, "This is the happiest baby on the planet!" At dusk the sun put on a spectacular fiery, multicolored display, full of power, inspiration, and glory.

After returning home everyone needed to rest. Meanwhile the moon was rising. The baby, being drowsy, was put to bed. The New York family kissed her good night, and goodbye. It was a very short trip, but Alex and Gabi had to return to school. It had been a meaningful, profound, and delightful trip. And after thanking their California family for their hospitality, they went back to their hotel.

Printed in the United States
By Bookmasters